M
Dictionary

CONTENTS

Major, Minor, 7th, 9th, Augmented,
Diminished, Major 6th, Minor 6th,
Major 7th, Minor 7th, 7th with
Augmented 5th, 7th with
Diminished 5th.

CHORD SYMBOLS

Major Chords = letter-name of the chord only.

Minor Chords = small m (or mi) following the
    letter-name of the chord.

Seventh Chords = 7 following the letter-name of
    the chord.

Ninth Chords = 9 following the letter-name of
    the chord.

Augmented Chords = + (or Aug. or +5) following
    the letter-name of the chord. They are named
    after any note of the chord.

Diminished Chords = — (or ° or dim.) following the
    letter-name of the chord. They are named
    after any note of the chord.

Major Sixth Chords = 6 (or M6) following the
    letter-name of the chord.

Minor Sixth Chords = m6 (or mi6) following the
    letter-name of the chord.

Major Seventh Chords = maj7 (or ma7 or M7)
    following the letter-name of the chord.

Minor Seventh Chords = m7 (or mi7) following the
    letter-name of the chord.

Seventh Chords with Augmented Fifth = 7+5
    (or 7aug5 or 7+ or aug7) following the
    letter-name of the chord.

Seventh Chords with Diminished Fifth = 7—5
    (or 7♭5 or 7°5) following the letter-name
    of the chord.

Second Edition
Copyright © MCMXCII by Alfred Publishing Co., Inc.

THE MANDOLIN

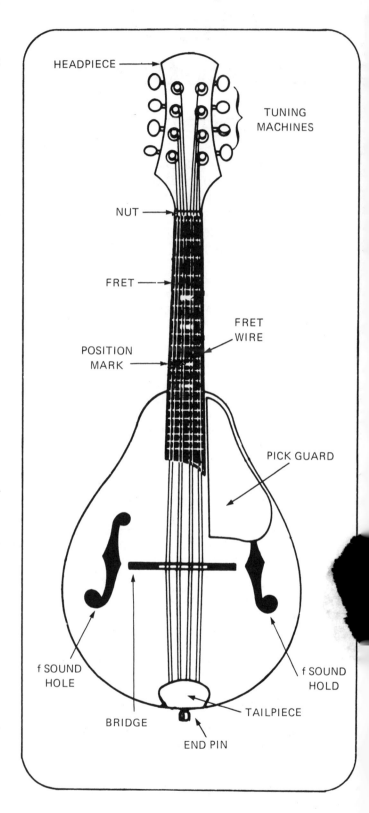

HEADPIECE

TUNING MACHINES

NUT

FRET

FRET WIRE

POSITION MARK

PICK GUARD

f SOUND HOLE

f SOUND HOLD

BRIDGE

TAILPIECE

END PIN

HOW TO HOLD
YOUR MANDOLIN

When playing, keep your left wrist away from the fingerboard. This will allow your fingers to be in a better position to finger the chords. Press your fingers firmly, but make certain they do not touch the neighboring strings.

Getting Acquainted With Music

Musical sounds are indicated by symbols called NOTES. Their time value is determined by their color (white or black) and by stems and flags attached to the note:

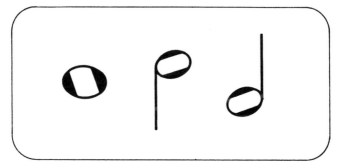

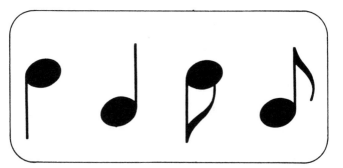

The notes are named after the first seven letters of the alphabet (A-G), endlessly repeated to embrace the entire range of musical sound. The name and pitch of the note is determined by its position on five horizontal lines, and the spaces between, called the . . .

STAFF

5th LINE - F	
	4th SPACE - E
4th LINE - D	
	3rd SPACE - C
3rd LINE - B	
	2nd SPACE - A
2nd LINE - G	
	1st SPACE - F
1st LINE - E	

NOTES ON THE LINES

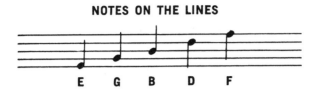

E   G   B   D   F

NOTES IN THE SPACES

F   A   C   E

Music is also divided into equal parts, called . . .

MEASURES

One measure is divided from another by

a BAR LINE

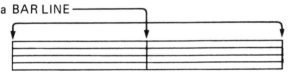

During the evolution of musical notation, the staff had from 2 to 20 lines, and symbols were invented to locate certain lines and the pitch of the note on that line. These symbols were called . . .

CLEFS

Music has three clefs, the C, F and G clefs. The entire range of the Mandolin can be written in the G clef. Originally the Gothic letter G was used on a four-line staff to establish the pitch of G:

It grew into the modern

G

Comparative Note Values

The WHOLE NOTE

receives 4 BEATS
(4 counts).

The DOTTED HALF NOTE

receives 3 BEATS.

The HALF NOTE

receives 2 BEATS.

The DOTTED QUARTER NOTE

receives 1½ BEATS.

The QUARTER NOTE

receives 1 BEAT.

The EIGHTH NOTE

receives 1/2 BEAT.

Measures

Music is divided into equal parts called MEASURES. A BAR LINE divides one measure from another.

BAR LINE   BAR LINE   double bar line means the end.

| ONE MEASURE | ONE MEASURE |

To indicate the number of beats in each measure, we use a . . .

Time Signature

The Time Signature

$\frac{2}{4}$ $\frac{3}{4}$ $\frac{4}{4}$ $\frac{6}{8}$ ← beats in each measure,

means

← and note getting one beat.

For each note value, there is a comparative REST sign.

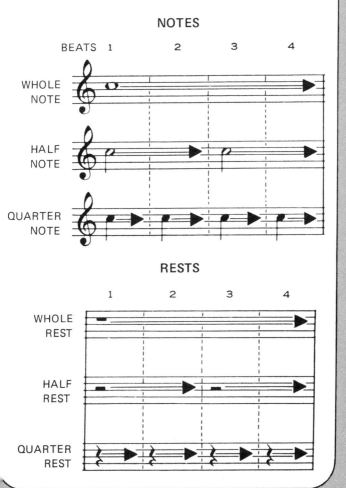

NOTES

| BEATS | 1 | 2 | 3 | 4 |

WHOLE NOTE

HALF NOTE

QUARTER NOTE

RESTS

| | 1 | 2 | 3 | 4 |

WHOLE REST

HALF REST

QUARTER REST

HOW TO TUNE
YOUR MANDOLIN

The strings of your mandolin are the same pitch as the four notes shown on the piano in the following illustration:

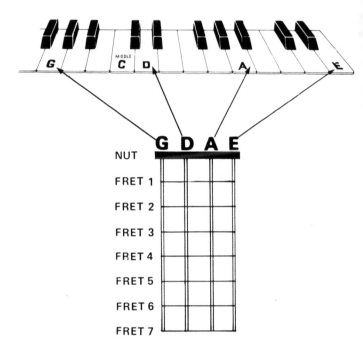

Pitch pipes are also useful for tuning and are available at your local music store or studio.

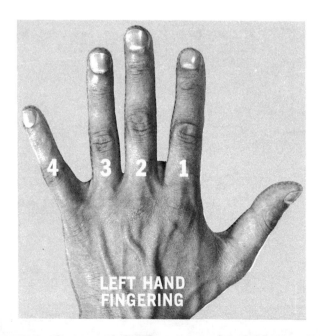

OTHER WAYS OF TUNING YOUR MANDOLIN

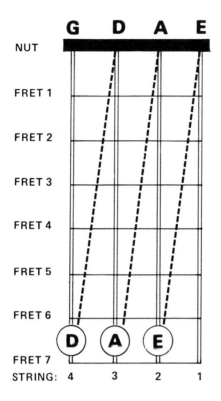

Tune the 4th string to G on the piano. If no piano is available, approximate G as best you can and proceed as follows:

- Press 7th fret of 4th string to equal pitch of 3rd string (D).

- Press 7th fret of 3rd string to equal pitch of 2nd string (A).

- Press 7th fret of 2nd string to equal pitch of 1st string (E).

CHORD CHART

If a string has an O over the string, it means it is an "open" string. It is strummed, but not fingered.

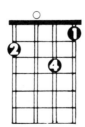

Numbers in circles represent finger numbers. Press down on the frets indicated with your left hand (see page 8) and strum the proper strings with your right.

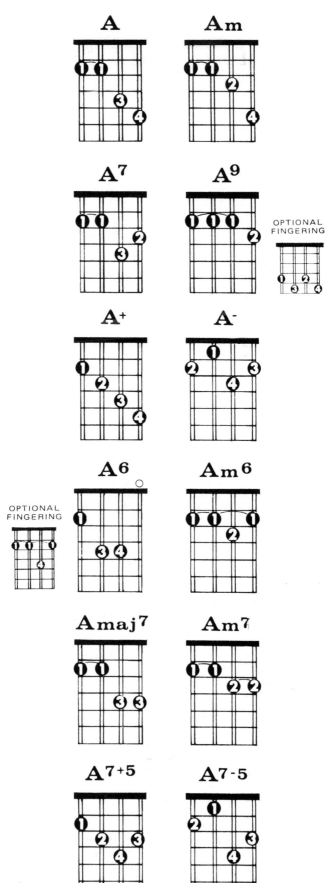

A

Am

A⁷

A⁹

OPTIONAL
FINGERING

A⁺

A⁻

OPTIONAL
FINGERING

A⁶

Am⁶

Amaj⁷

Am⁷

A⁷⁺⁵

A⁷⁻⁵

10

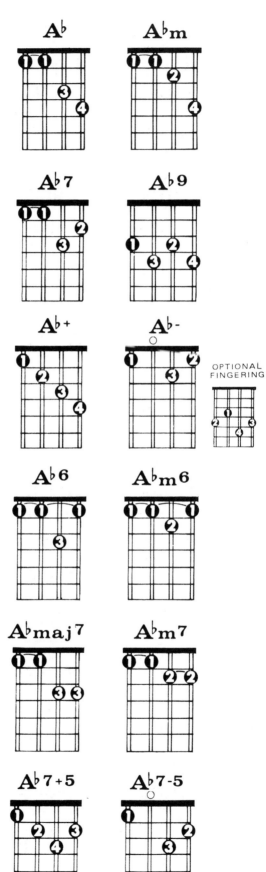

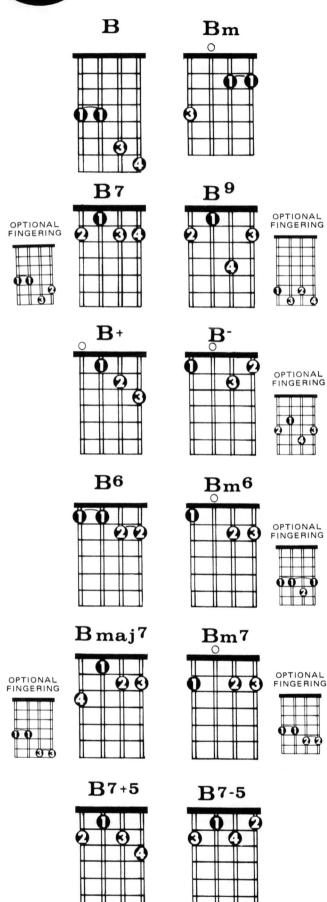

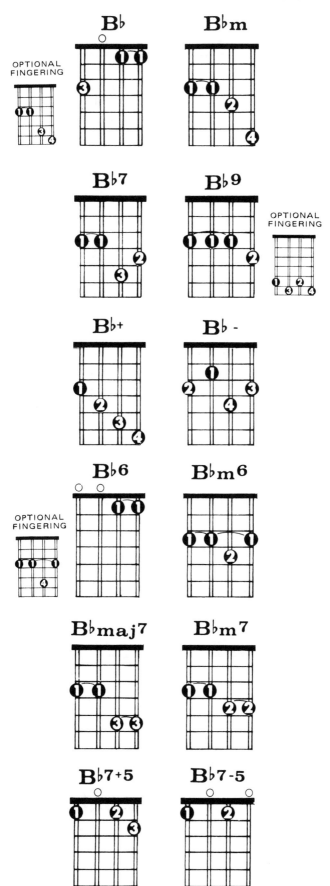

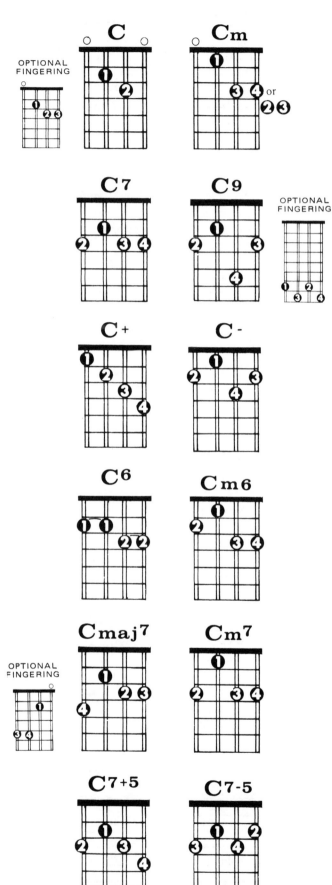

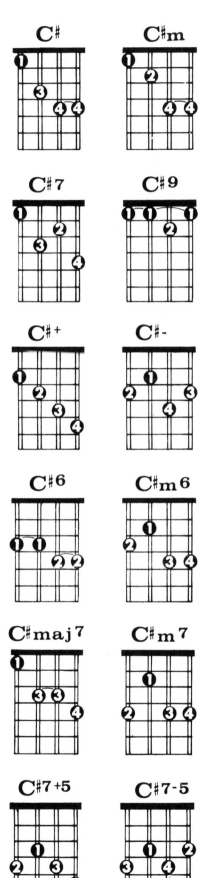

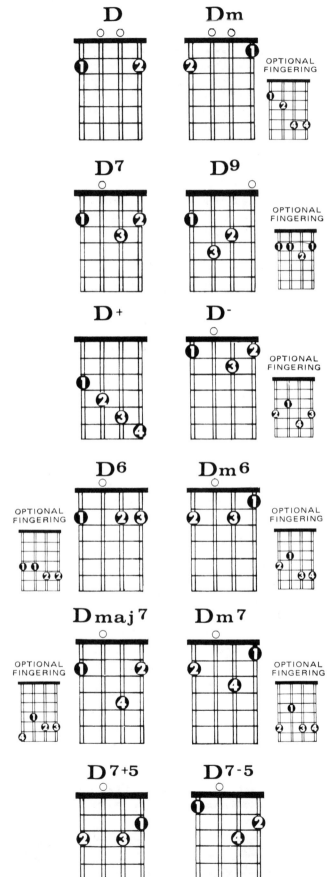

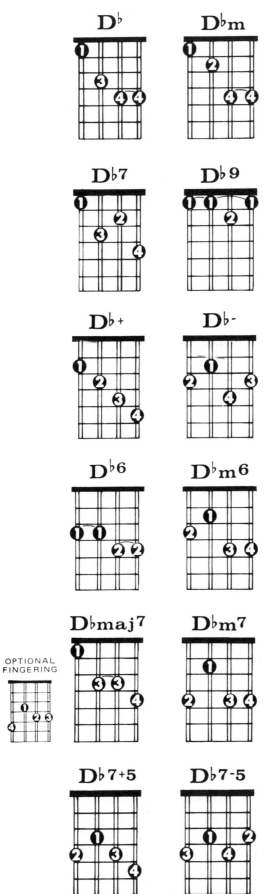

OPTIONAL
FINGERING

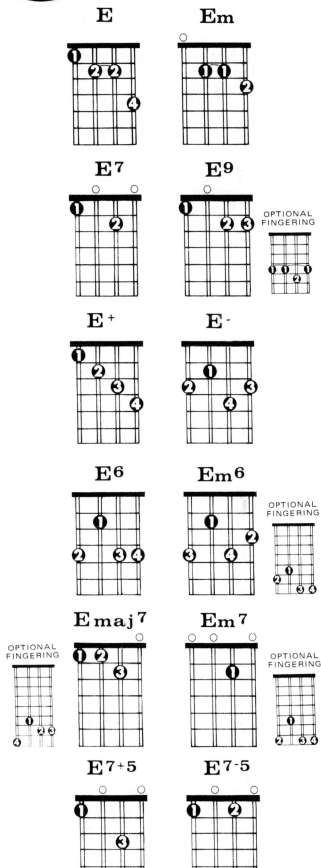

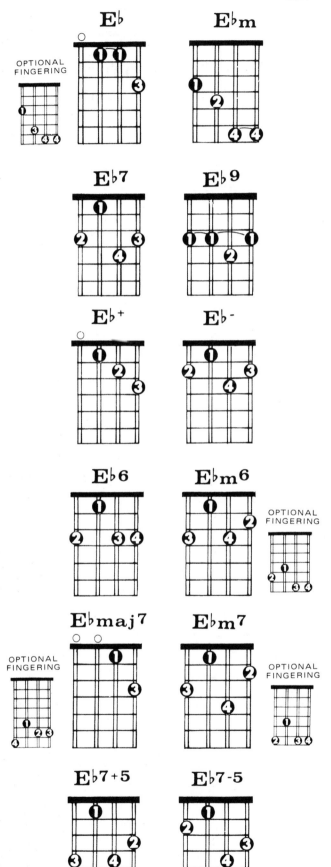

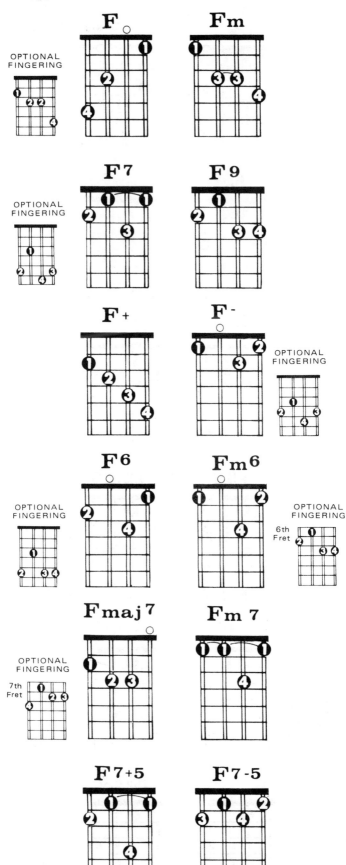

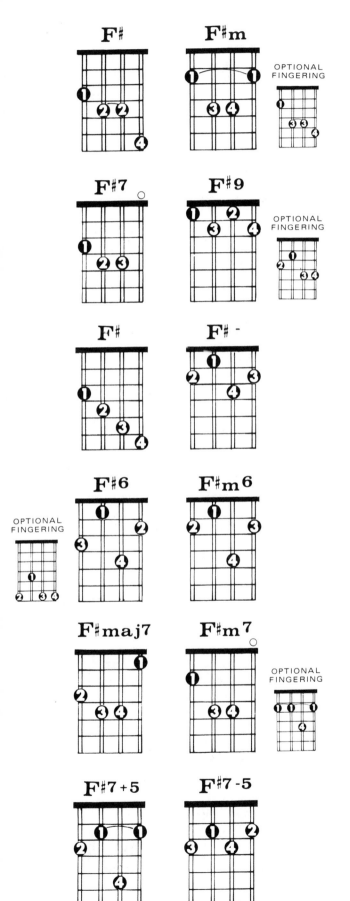

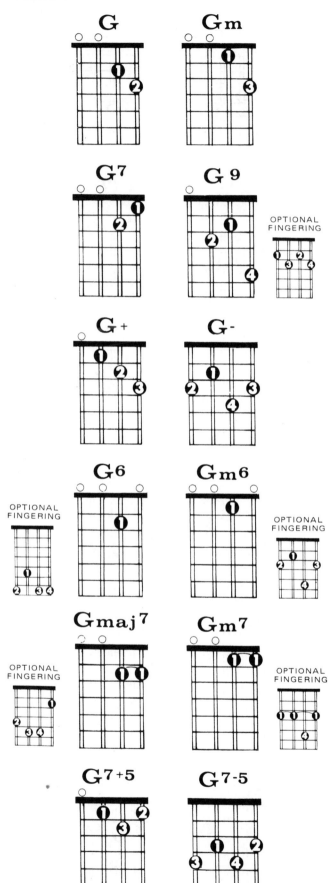

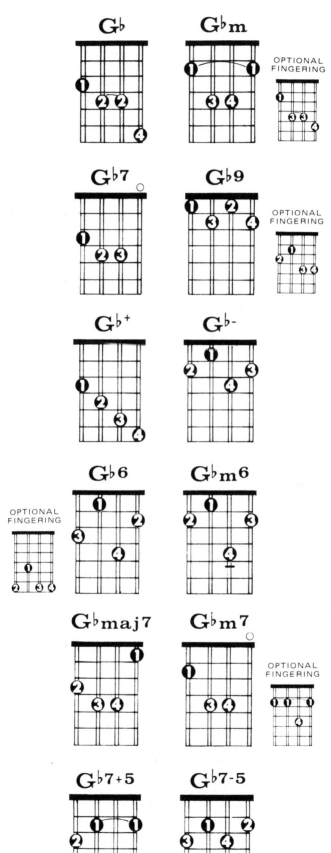

MOVABLE CHORD INTRODUCTION

Definitions

These chords are called "movable" because once a single fingering formation is learned, it can be moved up and down the fingerboard. In this way, a single fingering can be used for as many as twelve different chords.

A bar means to hold down two or more strings using only one finger. If the finger holds down all four strings, the bar is called "full".

Roots and Movable Chords

Every chord has a *root*. The root is the note that names the chord. For example, the root of an E major chord is the note E; the root of an A minor chord is the note A; the root of a C^7 chord is the note C, and so on.

When using movable chords, it is important to remember that, regardless of the fret on which the chord is played, *the root always remains on the same string*.

In the example below, the root of the A♭ major chord is A♭. This note is found on the 4th string.

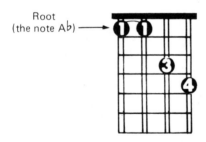

Since the name of the note on the 4th string is A♭, and since we started with a movable form of a *major* chord, the name of this chord is A♭ major. If we move the chord up one more fret, the root is still found on the 4th string. The note is A and the chord is now the A major chord.

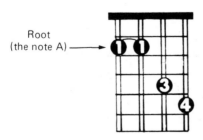

MOVABLE
MAJOR CHORD

With the root on the 4th string

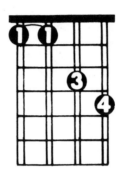

WITH BAR ACROSS THE 1st   FRET = A♭(G♯)
WITH BAR ACROSS THE 2nd FRET = A
WITH BAR ACROSS THE 3rd   FRET = B♭(A♯)
WITH BAR ACROSS THE 4th   FRET = B
WITH BAR ACROSS THE 5th   FRET = C
WITH BAR ACROSS THE 6th   FRET = D♭(C♯)
WITH BAR ACROSS THE 7th   FRET = D
WITH BAR ACROSS THE 8th   FRET = E♭(D♯)
WITH BAR ACROSS THE 9th   FRET = E
WITH BAR ACROSS THE 10th FRET = F
WITH BAR ACROSS THE 11th FRET = F♯(G♭)
WITH BAR ACROSS THE 12th FRET = G

MOVABLE
MAJOR CHORD

With the root on the 3rd string

Root on 3rd string

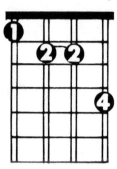

WITH BAR ACROSS THE 1st FRET = E

WITH BAR ACROSS THE 2nd FRET = F

WITH BAR ACROSS THE 3rd FRET = F♯ (G♭)

WITH BAR ACROSS THE 4th FRET = G

WITH BAR ACROSS THE 5th FRET = A♭ (G♯)

WITH BAR ACROSS THE 6th FRET = A

WITH BAR ACROSS THE 7th FRET = B♭ (A♯)

WITH BAR ACROSS THE 8th FRET = B

WITH BAR ACROSS THE 9th FRET = C

WITH BAR ACROSS THE 10th FRET = D♭ (C♯)

WITH BAR ACROSS THE 11th FRET = D

WITH BAR ACROSS THE 12th FRET = E♭ (D♯)

MOVABLE
MAJOR CHORD

With the root on the 2nd string

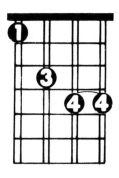

WITH BAR ACROSS THE 1st   FRET = D♭ (C♯)
WITH BAR ACROSS THE 2nd FRET = D
WITH BAR ACROSS THE 3rd   FRET = E♭ (D♯)
WITH BAR ACROSS THE 4th   FRET = E
WITH BAR ACROSS THE 5th   FRET = F
WITH BAR ACROSS THE 6th   FRET = F♯ (G♭)
WITH BAR ACROSS THE 7th   FRET = G
WITH BAR ACROSS THE 8th   FRET = A♭ (G♯)
WITH BAR ACROSS THE 9th   FRET = A
WITH BAR ACROSS THE 10th FRET = B♭ (A♯)
WITH BAR ACROSS THE 11th FRET = B
WITH BAR ACROSS THE 12th FRET = C

MOVABLE
MINOR CHORD

With the root on the 4th string

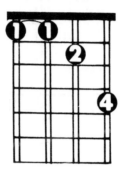

WITH BAR ACROSS THE 1st   FRET = A♭m (G♯)
WITH BAR ACROSS THE 2nd FRET = Am
WITH BAR ACROSS THE 3rd   FRET = B♭m (A♯)
WITH BAR ACROSS THE 4th   FRET = Bm
WITH BAR ACROSS THE 5th   FRET = Cm
WITH BAR ACROSS THE 6th   FRET = D♭m (C♯)
WITH BAR ACROSS THE 7th   FRET = Dm
WITH BAR ACROSS THE 8th   FRET = E♭m (D♯)
WITH BAR ACROSS THE 9th   FRET = Em
WITH BAR ACROSS THE 10th FRET = Fm
WITH BAR ACROSS THE 11th FRET = F♯m (G♭)
WITH BAR ACROSS THE 12th FRET = Gm

MOVABLE
MINOR CHORD

With the root on the 3rd string

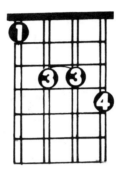

WITH BAR ACROSS THE 1st   FRET = Fm
WITH BAR ACROSS THE 2nd   FRET = F#m (G♭)
WITH BAR ACROSS THE 3rd   FRET = Gm
WITH BAR ACROSS THE 4th   FRET = A♭m (G#)
WITH BAR ACROSS THE 5th   FRET = Am
WITH BAR ACROSS THE 6th   FRET = B♭m (A#)
WITH BAR ACROSS THE 7th   FRET = Bm
WITH BAR ACROSS THE 8th   FRET = Cm
WITH BAR ACROSS THE 9th   FRET = D♭m (C#)
WITH BAR ACROSS THE 10th FRET = Dm
WITH BAR ACROSS THE 11th FRET = E♭m (D#)
WITH BAR ACROSS THE 12th FRET = Em

MOVABLE
MINOR CHORD

With the root on the 2nd string

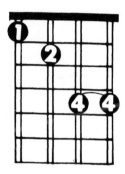

WITH BAR ACROSS THE 1st   FRET = D♭m (C♯)

WITH BAR ACROSS THE 2nd FRET = Dm

WITH BAR ACROSS THE 3rd   FRET = E♭m (D♯)

WITH BAR ACROSS THE 4th   FRET = Em

WITH BAR ACROSS THE 5th   FRET = Fm

WITH BAR ACROSS THE 6th   FRET = F♯m (G♭)

WITH BAR ACROSS THE 7th   FRET = Gm

WITH BAR ACROSS THE 8th   FRET = A♭m (G♯)

WITH BAR ACROSS THE 9th   FRET = Am

WITH BAR ACROSS THE 10th FRET = B♭m (A♯)

WITH BAR ACROSS THE 11th FRET = Bm

WITH BAR ACROSS THE 12th FRET = Cm

MOVABLE
7th CHORD

With the root on the 4th string

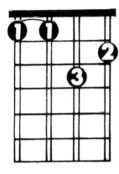 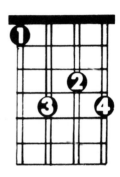

WITH BAR ACROSS THE 1st   FRET = Ab^7 (G$\sharp$)
WITH BAR ACROSS THE 2nd FRET = A^7
WITH BAR ACROSS THE 3rd   FRET = Bb (A$\sharp$)
WITH BAR ACROSS THE 4th   FRET = B^7
WITH BAR ACROSS THE 5th   FRET = C^7
WITH BAR ACROSS THE 6th   FRET = Db^7 (C$\sharp$)
WITH BAR ACROSS THE 7th   FRET = D^7
WITH BAR ACROSS THE 8th   FRET = Eb^7 (D$\sharp$)
WITH BAR ACROSS THE 9th   FRET = E^7
WITH BAR ACROSS THE 10th FRET = F^7
WITH BAR ACROSS THE 11th FRET = $F\sharp^7$ (Gb)
WITH BAR ACROSS THE 12th FRET = G^7

MOVABLE
7th CHORD

With the root on the 3rd string

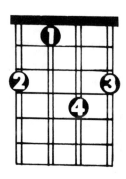

WITH BAR ACROSS THE 1st   FRET = E$\flat^7$ (D$\sharp$)

WITH BAR ACROSS THE 2nd FRET = E^7

WITH BAR ACROSS THE 3rd   FRET = F^7

WITH BAR ACROSS THE 4th   FRET = F$\sharp^7$ (G$\flat$)

WITH BAR ACROSS THE 5th   FRET = G^7

WITH BAR ACROSS THE 6th   FRET = A$\flat^7$ (G$\sharp$)

WITH BAR ACROSS THE 7th   FRET = A^7

WITH BAR ACROSS THE 8th   FRET = B$\flat^7$ (A$\sharp$)

WITH BAR ACROSS THE 9th   FRET = B^7

WITH BAR ACROSS THE 10th FRET = C^7

WITH BAR ACROSS THE 11th FRET = D$\flat^7$ (C$\sharp$)

WITH BAR ACROSS THE 12th FRET = D^7

MOVABLE
7th CHORD

With the root on the 2nd string

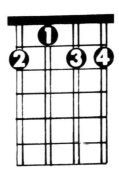

WITH BAR ACROSS THE 1st FRET = B^7
WITH BAR ACROSS THE 2nd FRET = C^7
WITH BAR ACROSS THE 3rd FRET = D$\flat^7$ (C$\sharp$)
WITH BAR ACROSS THE 4th FRET = D^7
WITH BAR ACROSS THE 5th FRET = E$\flat^7$ (D$\sharp$)
WITH BAR ACROSS THE 6th FRET = E^7
WITH BAR ACROSS THE 7th FRET = F^7
WITH BAR ACROSS THE 8th FRET = F$\sharp^7$ (G$\flat$)
WITH BAR ACROSS THE 9th FRET = G^7
WITH BAR ACROSS THE 10th FRET = A$\flat^7$ (G$\sharp$)
WITH BAR ACROSS THE 11th FRET = A^7
WITH BAR ACROSS THE 12th FRET = B$\flat^7$ (A$\sharp$)

MOVABLE
9th CHORD

With the root on the 1st string

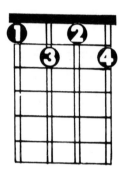

WITH BAR ACROSS THE 1st FRET = $F\sharp^9$ (G♭)
WITH BAR ACROSS THE 2nd FRET = G^9
WITH BAR ACROSS THE 3rd FRET = $A♭^9$ (G♯)
WITH BAR ACROSS THE 4th FRET = A^9
WITH BAR ACROSS THE 5th FRET = $B♭^9$ (A♯)
WITH BAR ACROSS THE 6th FRET = B^9
WITH BAR ACROSS THE 7th FRET = C^9
WITH BAR ACROSS THE 8th FRET = $D♭^9$ (C♯)
WITH BAR ACROSS THE 9th FRET = D^9
WITH BAR ACROSS THE 10th FRET = $E♭^9$ (D♯)
WITH BAR ACROSS THE 11th FRET = E^9
WITH BAR ACROSS THE 12th FRET = F^9

MOVABLE
6th CHORD

With the root on the 4th string

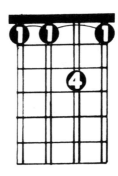

WITH BAR ACROSS THE 1st   FRET = Ab^6 (G#)
WITH BAR ACROSS THE 2nd FRET = A^6
WITH BAR ACROSS THE 3rd   FRET = Bb^6 (C#)
WITH BAR ACROSS THE 4th   FRET = B^6
WITH BAR ACROSS THE 5th   FRET = C^6
WITH BAR ACROSS THE 6th   FRET = Db^6 (C#)
WITH BAR ACROSS THE 7th   FRET = D^6
WITH BAR ACROSS THE 8th   FRET = Eb^6 (D#)
WITH BAR ACROSS THE 9th   FRET = E^6
WITH BAR ACROSS THE 10th FRET = F^6
WITH BAR ACROSS THE 11th FRET = $F#^6$ (Gb)
WITH BAR ACROSS THE 12th FRET = G^6

MOVABLE
6th CHORD

With the root on the 3rd string

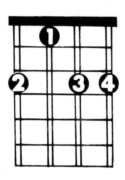

WITH BAR ACROSS THE 1st   FRET = E♭⁶ (D#)
WITH BAR ACROSS THE 2nd FRET = E⁶
WITH BAR ACROSS THE 3rd   FRET = F⁶
WITH BAR ACROSS THE 4th   FRET = F#⁶ (G♭)
WITH BAR ACROSS THE 5th   FRET = G⁶
WITH BAR ACROSS THE 6th   FRET = A♭⁶ (G#)
WITH BAR ACROSS THE 7th   FRET = A⁶
WITH BAR ACROSS THE 8th   FRET = B♭⁶ (A#)
WITH BAR ACROSS THE 9th   FRET = B⁶
WITH BAR ACROSS THE 10th FRET = C⁶
WITH BAR ACROSS THE 11th FRET = D♭⁶ (C#)
WITH BAR ACROSS THE 12th FRET = D⁶

MOVABLE
6th CHORD

With the root on the 2nd string

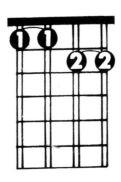

WITH BAR ACROSS THE 1st FRET = B^6

WITH BAR ACROSS THE 2nd FRET = C^6

WITH BAR ACROSS THE 3rd FRET = $D\flat^6$ (C♯)

WITH BAR ACROSS THE 4th FRET = D^6

WITH BAR ACROSS THE 5th FRET = $E\flat^6$ (D♯)

WITH BAR ACROSS THE 6th FRET = E^6

WITH BAR ACROSS THE 7th FRET = F^6

WITH BAR ACROSS THE 8th FRET = $F♯^6$ (G♭)

WITH BAR ACROSS THE 9th FRET = G^6

WITH BAR ACROSS THE 10th FRET = $A\flat^6$ (G♯)

WITH BAR ACROSS THE 11th FRET = A^6

WITH BAR ACROSS THE 12th FRET = $B\flat^6$ (A♯)

MOVABLE MINOR 6th CHORD

With the root on the 4th string

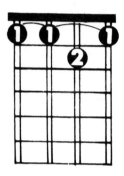

WITH BAR ACROSS THE 1st   FRET = A♭(G♯)
WITH BAR ACROSS THE 2nd FRET = A
WITH BAR ACROSS THE 3rd FRET = B♭(A♯)
WITH BAR ACROSS THE 4th   FRET = B
WITH BAR ACROSS THE 5th   FRET = C
WITH BAR ACROSS THE 6th   FRET = D♭(C♯)
WITH BAR ACROSS THE 7th   FRET = D
WITH BAR ACROSS THE 8th   FRET = E♭(D♯)
WITH BAR ACROSS THE 9th   FRET = E
WITH BAR ACROSS THE 10th FRET = F
WITH BAR ACROSS THE 11th FRET = F♯(G♭)
WITH BAR ACROSS THE 12th FRET = G

MOVABLE
MINOR
6th CHORD

With the root on the 2nd string

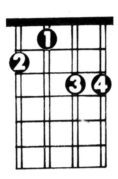

WITH BAR ACROSS THE 1st   FRET = C

WITH BAR ACROSS THE 2nd   FRET = D♭(C♯)

WITH BAR ACROSS THE 3rd   FRET = D

WITH BAR ACROSS THE 4th   FRET = E♭(D♯)

WITH BAR ACROSS THE 5th   FRET = E

WITH BAR ACROSS THE 6th   FRET = F

WITH BAR ACROSS THE 7th   FRET = F♯(G♭)

WITH BAR ACROSS THE 8th   FRET = G

WITH BAR ACROSS THE 9th   FRET = A♭(G♯)

WITH BAR ACROSS THE 10th FRET = A

WITH BAR ACROSS THE 11th FRET = B♭(A♯)

WITH BAR ACROSS THE 12th FRET = B

MOVABLE
MAJOR
7th CHORD

With the root on the 4th string

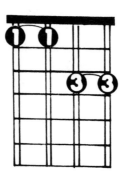

WITH BAR ACROSS THE 1st   FRET = A (G#)
WITH BAR ACROSS THE 2nd FRET = A
WITH BAR ACROSS THE 3rd   FRET = B♭(A#)
WITH BAR ACROSS THE 4th   FRET = B
WITH BAR ACROSS THE 5th   FRET = C
WITH BAR ACROSS THE 6th   FRET = D♭(C#)
WITH BAR ACROSS THE 7th   FRET = D
WITH BAR ACROSS THE 8th   FRET = E♭(D#)
WITH BAR ACROSS THE 9th   FRET = E
WITH BAR ACROSS THE 10th FRET = F
WITH BAR ACROSS THE 11th FRET = F#(G♭)
WITH BAR ACROSS THE 12th FRET = G

MOVABLE MAJOR 7th CHORD

With the root on the 2nd string

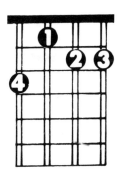

WITH BAR ACROSS THE 1st FRET = B
WITH BAR ACROSS THE 2nd FRET = C
WITH BAR ACROSS THE 3rd FRET = D♭(C♯)
WITH BAR ACROSS THE 4th FRET = D
WITH BAR ACROSS THE 5th FRET = E♭(D♯)
WITH BAR ACROSS THE 6th FRET = E
WITH BAR ACROSS THE 7th FRET = F
WITH BAR ACROSS THE 8th FRET = F♯(G♭)
WITH BAR ACROSS THE 9th FRET = G
WITH BAR ACROSS THE 10th FRET = A♭(G♯)
WITH BAR ACROSS THE 11th FRET = A
WITH BAR ACROSS THE 12th FRET = B♭(A♯)

MOVABLE
MINOR
7th CHORD

With the root on the 4th string

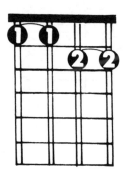

WITH BAR ACROSS THE 1st   FRET = A♭(G♯)
WITH BAR ACROSS THE 2nd FRET = A
WITH BAR ACROSS THE 3rd FRET = B♭(A♯)
WITH BAR ACROSS THE 4th   FRET = B
WITH BAR ACROSS THE 5th   FRET = C
WITH BAR ACROSS THE 6th   FRET = D♭(C♯)
WITH BAR ACROSS THE 7th   FRET = D
WITH BAR ACROSS THE 8th   FRET = E♭(D♯)
WITH BAR ACROSS THE 9th   FRET = E
WITH BAR ACROSS THE 10th FRET = F
WITH BAR ACROSS THE 11th FRET = F♯(G♭)
WITH BAR ACROSS THE 12th FRET = G

MOVABLE MINOR 7th CHORD

With the root on the 2nd string

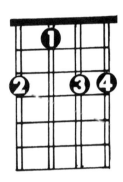

WITH BAR ACROSS THE 1st   FRET = C
WITH BAR ACROSS THE 2nd   FRET = D♭(C♯)
WITH BAR ACROSS THE 3rd   FRET = D
WITH BAR ACROSS THE 4th   FRET = E♭(D♯)
WITH BAR ACROSS THE 5th   FRET = E
WITH BAR ACROSS THE 6th   FRET = F
WITH BAR ACROSS THE 7th   FRET = F♯(G♭)
WITH BAR ACROSS THE 8th   FRET = G
WITH BAR ACROSS THE 9th   FRET = A♭(G♯)
WITH BAR ACROSS THE 10th   FRET = A
WITH BAR ACROSS THE 11th   FRET = B♭(A♯)
WITH BAR ACROSS THE 12th   FRET = B

MANDOLIN

The number in the black circle

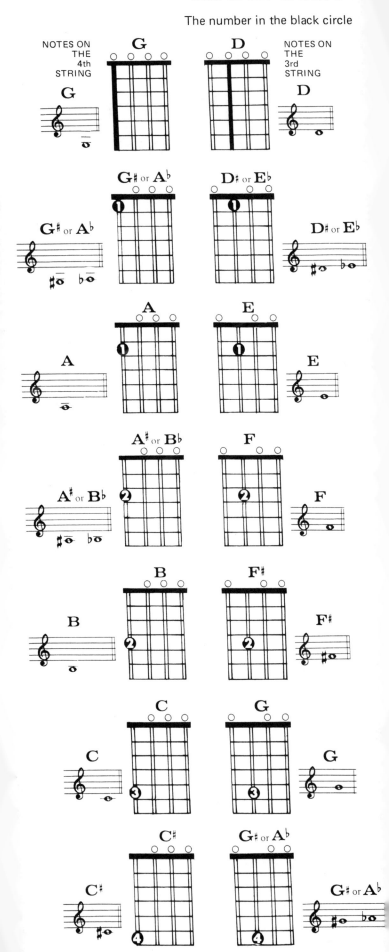

NOTE CHART

indicates the correct fingering.

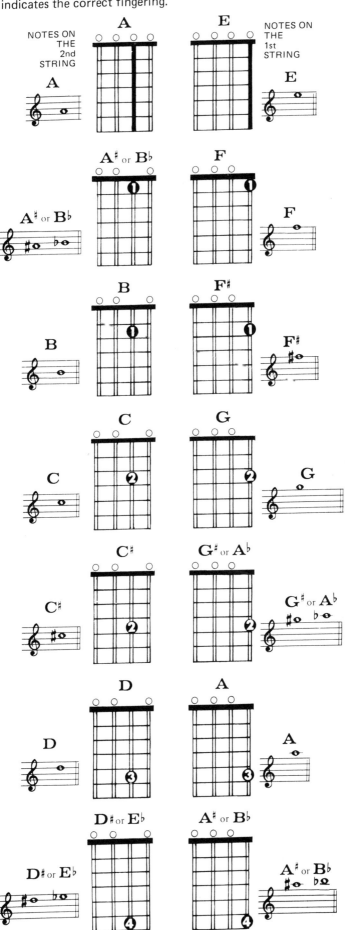

MAGIC CHORD

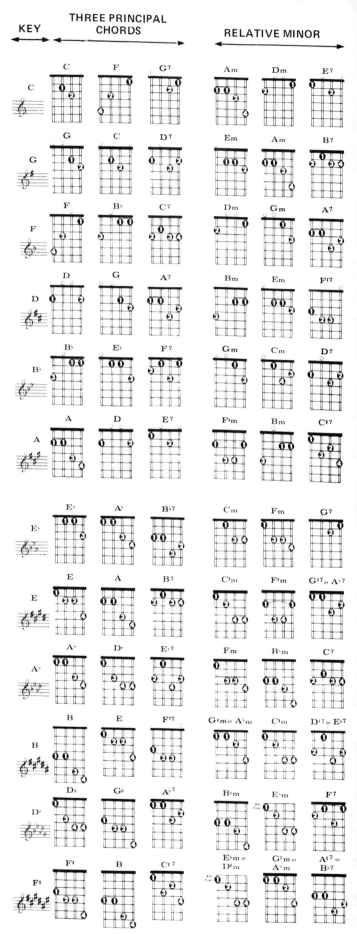

ACCOMPANIMENT GUIDE

ALTERNATE CHORDS

Numbers indicate fingering
O = Open
1 = Index finger   3 = Ring finger
2 = Middle finger   4 = Pinky

Chord Derivations

Chords are derived from the notes of the major scale. The chart below indicates which notes of the scale make up each chord. A ♭ means to lower the scale note by one fret; a ♯ means to raise the scale note by one fret; a ♭♭ means to lower the scale note by two frets.

CHORD	Notes of the Major Scale				
Major	1	3	5		
Minor	1	♭3	5		
7th	1	3	5	♭7	
9th	1	3	5	♭7	9
Augmented	1	3	♯5		
Diminished	1	♭3	♭5		
Major 6	1	3	5	6	
Minor 6	1	♭3	5	6	
Major 7	1	3	5	7	
Minor 7	1	♭3	5	♭7	
7th with Aug. 5	1	3	♯5	♭7	
7th with Dim. 5	1	3	♭5	♭7	

Major Keys and Relative Minors

MAJOR KEY	RELATIVE MINOR KEY	KEY SIGNATURE
A♭	F	4♭
A	F♯	3♯
B♭	G	2♭
B	G♯	5♯
C♭	A♭	7♭
C	A	NO♯ NO♭
C♯	A♯	7♯
D♭	B♭	5♭
D	B	2♯
E♭	C	3♭
E	C♯	4♯
F	D	1♭
F♯	D♯	6♯
G♭	E♭	6♭
G	E	1♯